NEW   EM

Guns and Violence

Gail B. Stewart

KidHaven Press, an imprint of Gale Group, Inc.

10911 Technology Place, San Diego, CA 92127

Library of Congress Cataloging-in-Publication Data

Stewart, Gail B., 1949–
      Guns and violence / by Gail B. Stewart.
         p. cm. — (Understanding issues)
      Includes bibliographical references.
      Summary: Discusses violence and its causes in schools and among gangs.
      The availability of guns, programs and laws designed to curb their use,
      and the impact of violence on the community are also discussed.
      ISBN 0-7377-0952-9 (acid-free)
      1. Violence. 2. Firearms. 3. School violence. I. Title. II. Series.
      HM1116 .S74 2002
      371. 7'82—dc21

      2001003361

Picture Credits

Cover photo: © Charles Gupton/The Stock Market
© AFP/CORBIS, 5, 7, 11, 18, 27, 28, 39
Associated Press, AP, 23, 26
© Philip James Corwin/CORBIS, 20
© Eye Ubiquitous/CORBIS, 30
© Robert Maass/CORBIS, 14
© Neal Preston/CORBIS, 33
© Reflections Photolibrary/CORBIS, 36
© Reuters NewMedia Inc./CORBIS, 17, 24, 35
© David & Peter Turnley/CORBIS, 8, 10, 15, 38

Printed in the U.S.A.

Contents

"As Fast as a Bullet Can Go"

Just after school began one morning in March, 2001, some students heard loud pops. The noise was coming from the courtyard outside their Santee, California, high school. Some thought it was firecrackers, and they wanted to see what was happening.

But it was not firecrackers. There were kids lying on the ground, bleeding. And the students could still hear the popping sound. Inside, in the boys' bathroom, more students were shot. After six minutes of shooting, the fifteen-year-old boy gave up his gun to the police.

He was a small, shy boy kids called Andy. He did not look like a violent person. He did not seem like a boy who would kill anyone. But that morning, he shot fifteen students and two of them died.

Very quickly, reporters from newspapers and television stations came to the school. They interviewed people, and asked them what had happened. Everyone wanted to understand where Charles "Andy"

Andy Williams shot fifteen students at a Santee, California, high school.

Williams had gotten a gun. And why, they asked, did he decide to use it to shoot and kill his classmates?

More Violence Follows

The shooting at this high school was upsetting to people throughout the country. However, it was not the only gun violence that involved young people at the time. Within a week of that shooting, a number of other stories about guns made the news. In a Seattle classroom, a boy pulled out a gun and threatened his teacher and classmates. In Pennsylvania, a fourteen-year-old girl shot another girl in the arm as she sat in the school lunchroom. In New York City, four teenagers with shotguns killed a store owner.

Some of the stories were about young people who had made plans to shoot guns. In California, two boys had a gun and a **"hit list."** The list named the people they planned on killing. A fifteen-year-old in New Jersey made threats to kill a number of students, too. One story was about an eight-year-old boy who was arrested at his Philadelphia school. He told people he was going to cause a "bloodbath" with his shotgun.

Too Easy

All of these stories are frightening. Parents want their children to be safe. They don't want them around guns. They don't want their children's names on hit lists, either.

"If I found out Paul's name was on a list like that, I don't think I would let him go to school," says one

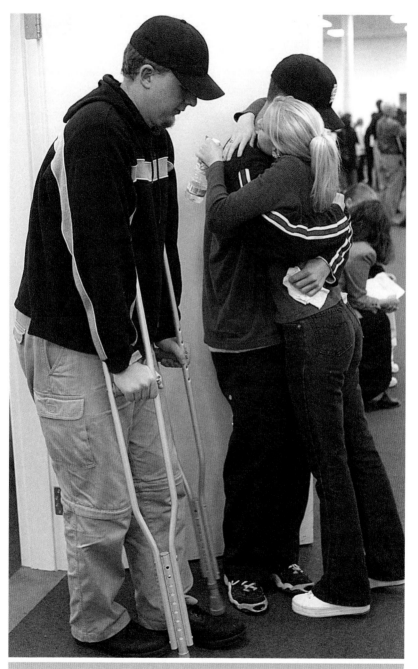

A student wounded by a high school shooter.

Gun violence ruins many lives.

mother. "Even if the one with the list said he was just pretending, how could I take a chance like that?"[1]

Other parents agree. "Just knowing there was a kid with a gun who lived in our neighborhood or went to the same school would be terrifying," says one father. "You teach your kids right and wrong. You know they have good friends with nice parents. But then some kid who is angry about something just decides to shoot him? That's the scariest thing I can imagine."[2]

It seems that there are more and more stories in which a loaded gun is in the hands of a teen or child. Many of these stories end in tragedy. Every day, about fifteen teens or younger children die from gunshot wounds in the United States—more than fifty-four hundred each year. In fact, the murder rate for teens between thirteen and seventeen is at an all-time high. Tragedies like these hurt entire families.

"As fast as a bullet can go," says one man, whose fourteen-year-old grandson died after being shot by a gang member, "that's how quick a future can end. That's how quick I stopped being somebody's grandpa."[3]

Not on Purpose

Not all the guns were fired on purpose. Fifteen children in the United States die each month from accidental shootings. About 130 each month are injured—and some of those injuries are very serious. One little girl found a small silver gun in her mother's purse. She thought it was a toy, and aimed it at her baby sister. When the gun went off, a bullet hit the baby in the foot.

Another accident ended in a sadder way. A fourteen-year-old Colorado boy named Patrick was at a party. His sister Chantay was there, too. She became worried when she saw Patrick and another boy looking at a gun. It belonged to the parents of the boy having the party. Chantay went over and

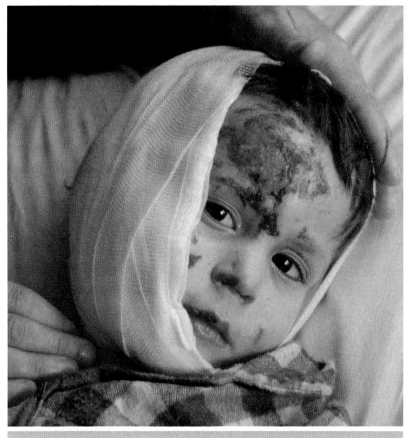

Accidental shootings happen every day.

tried to grab the gun away, and it went off. Patrick died before reaching the hospital.

The story took an even sadder turn. Even though it was not her fault, Chantay could not stop being sad. Her family remembers that Chantay felt so guilty that she often dreamed about the accident. Says her mother, "She would wake me up screaming, 'Mama, I can't get the blood off my hands!'"[4]

Therapists and doctors tried to help Chantay. Her parents tried to help, too. But she killed herself, three weeks after she accidentally shot her brother. That accident caused two deaths.

Other Dangers

Gun violence can happen by accident or on purpose. Often it results in death—that of a child or an adult. Some of those who die shoot themselves.

A victim of a school shooting.

One counselor worries that guns are too tempting when people are feeling bad. He believes that many suicides happen just because a person had a gun nearby.

"You put a gun in the hand of that guy, he's going to use it," he says. "He is not thinking clearly. He might be drinking or on drugs. If that gun wasn't there, would the guy get in his car and ride around to find one? I don't think he would. Not in every case. I think it is a spur of the moment thing sometimes. And the gun just makes it easier."[5]

Gun violence is a problem that needs to be solved now. Each day more and more young people are dying. Some of the shootings are accidental, some on purpose. Either way, so many lives are ruined.

One woman whose son was shot says she doesn't remember how it feels to be really happy. "I feel as if, when I lost my son, I lost the joy of living," she says sadly. "This is a different life than the one I had before."[6]

Chapter Two

The Wrong Hands

People own more guns than ever before. In 1994, 40 percent of homes with children in the United States had at least one gun. By 2000 that number had risen to 50 percent. Why are there so many guns?

Reasons for Owning Guns

There are a variety of reasons people own guns. Some use guns for hunting or for target shooting. Don Jakes, a retired shoe salesman, says he is hooked on target shooting.

"I never owned a gun before," he says. "But I have one now. A friend brought me to a target range, and I loved it. I don't think I could ever shoot a deer or anything, but targets are fun. That's what my gun is for."[7]

Other people collect guns from different times in history. One man says he has a collection of guns from World War II. Another says he and his brother collect weapons from the Civil War. They buy the guns at **auctions**. They are not used for shooting—merely for display.

Some people have guns because of the type of jobs they have. Police officers and many private investigators have guns. One man delivers large numbers of diamonds to jewelers. He carries them in a special briefcase that is locked to his wrist. He also carries a gun.

Some people use guns only for target shooting.

Some people own guns so that they feel safer.

"I have never had to use it," he says. "I hope I never do have to use it. But just in case—I have it in my pocket. I feel safer."[8]

Protection

Feeling safer is a very big reason people have guns. Even though they do not carry jewels or chase criminals, they do not feel safe. Sometimes it is because they live in a neighborhood where there is a lot of crime. That's the reason James's parents bought a gun.

"My dad got it off a guy he works with," says James. "I know why he bought it. There were some guys that were selling drugs near our [apartment] building. My dad called the man who owns the building. He complained about the drug sellers. He called the police, too.

"Those guys know it was my dad that complained. The police came around and talked to them, I think. But they haven't stopped selling drugs. They are mad at my dad, though. Every time he walks by them they say things. He's afraid they might hurt my mom or my little sisters to get back at him. So when they go outside, he walks with them. He has a gun in the pocket of his jacket."[9]

Mary has a gun, too. She got it after her husband Larry broke her arm and her nose. She and her two small children are on their own, and she worries that Larry will find them.

"He's hit me and my kids more times than I can count," she says. "I don't think I could ever really shoot him or anybody else. But if he comes around here, I'll wave this gun in his face. You bet I would. I've got to protect my family."[10]

Getting a Gun

There are 200 million guns in the United States. That's about one for every man, woman, and child. But even though there are plenty of guns, not everyone is allowed to own one. There are laws about the sale of guns and about who can

Dealers must do a background check and see proof of age before they sell a gun.

or cannot buy them. These laws differ from state to state.

In most states, a person must be twenty-one years old to purchase a handgun from a gun dealer. After seeing proof of age, the dealer must do a background check of the customer. It is illegal to sell a gun to anyone with a criminal record.

In some states, buyers must wait several days before getting their gun. This is to prevent people from rushing to gun stores to buy a gun when they are angry or upset. They cannot buy a gun on the spur of the moment. It is easy to see why this delay is sometimes called a **"cooling-off period."** Other states do not require a delay. A customer can get the gun after the gun dealer completes the **background check** which is administered by the Federal Bureau of Investigation (FBI).

Some unlicensed dealers will sell guns without checking age or background.

Other Ways to Get Guns

Not everyone buys guns from licensed gun dealers. Some people buy them at gun shows. Some of the dealers at a gun show are licensed, and they follow the rules about background checks and proof of age. However, there are some who are not licensed dealers. They sometimes sell to customers without checking—this is against the law.

One man (who did not want his name used) admits he has a criminal record. Even so, he was able to buy guns at a local gun show. He looked for a seller who was not licensed.

"I'd had a number of drunk driving arrests," he says. "And I served eighteen months in prison for burglary. So they'd find that out when they did a background check. I bought a rifle and a pistol from another guy at the show. He didn't have a booth; he was selling weapons out of his camper. He just took my money and told me to take it easy."[11]

Other people buy guns on the street. These are often stolen guns. The people who buy them are either criminals or those too young to buy a gun legally. It is not suprising that many of these guns are used to commit crimes. Unfortunately, these street dealers are only interested in making money—they don't care that what they are doing is illegal.

"You look out on Lake Street here," says one sixteen-year-old, pointing out his apartment window. "I can find seven or eight guys that will sell me a gun. Hey, I even got one real easy when I was eleven. If you got the cash, they'll set you right up."[12]

A Surprising Source

One Detroit newspaper did a survey in a middle school. More than 70 percent of the students said they were pretty sure that they could get an illegal gun in twenty-four hours. And one-third of those students said they could get a gun in less than three

Some parents do not lock guns away in a safe place.

hours. But when asked *where* they would get the gun, many students gave a surprising answer. It was not from a street dealer, or from a gun show. It was from their own homes.

Experts say that many parents are not careful with their guns. They do not lock them in a safe place where children cannot get to them. Sometimes these guns are loaded, and that is even more dangerous.

"I've had people say, 'I have to keep the gun loaded,'" says one police officer. "They say, 'If someone breaks in, an empty gun won't help me.' But then they put a loaded gun in a drawer by the bed, or someplace even a little kid could find. That's disaster, waiting to happen. If it's loaded, you have to keep it locked up and hidden."[13]

Whether young people find guns at home or buy them from a street dealer, the result is the same. Too many who should not have guns are armed. And they are very dangerous—to themselves and to others.

Chapter Three

Guns at School

"It makes me so sad," says one teacher. "I've watched so many stories on television about kids killing each other in schools. I just can't understand it. I mean, school is supposed to be a safe place. Kids aren't supposed to be afraid. No one should worry that they might be shot anyplace, but at school?"[14]

Bringing Guns to School

Unfortunately, schools are not always safe places. Guns and other weapons show up too often, say teachers. In a 1999 poll by the *Washington Post*, one-third of the students had heard another teen threaten to kill someone. Each day, more than 100,000 U.S. teens have a gun in their locker, purse, or backpack. Very few are caught. In fact, in the 1996–1997 school year, only six thousand students across the country were expelled for bringing guns.

Of course, most students who have guns do not intend to shoot their classmates. They insist that they have reasons for being armed. One twelve-year-old boy said he brought his brother's gun to school six or seven times and has never been caught with it.

"I brought it because I wanted to show some people," he shrugs. "I told my friends about the gun, but I don't think they believed me at first. But

These weapons were taken from students at school.

A memorial for victims of a school shooting.

I brought it and they saw it with their own eyes. It was cool."[15]

"It's Me and My Gun, or I'm Not Going"

Many students who bring guns say they are just protecting themselves. They have been threatened or attacked by others. Having a gun makes them feel safer.

Dewayne says that at his high school almost every one of his friends had guns. "The girls, too," he says. "My girlfriend got threatened by two guys last year. And so her brother gave her a gun. She keeps it in her backpack, loaded and everything."[16]

Many students say they don't care that bringing a gun is against the rules. They feel unsafe walking to school, or even in certain parts of the school building or grounds. Tara, seventeen, has been getting threatened at school. She doesn't have a gun now, but she wants to buy one.

"I've been skipping school a lot," says Tara. "There's this girl at school who keeps threatening me. She and her friends already stole my coat and everything in my locker. She told me she'll hurt me next time. So I've just been staying home. My mom doesn't know, because she leaves for work before me. I want to get a gun, because I'll be protected then. Otherwise, I'm not going to school. It's me and my gun, or I'm not going."[17]

Gang Violence

There are thousands of students like Tara who miss school because they are afraid. They have been threatened or hurt. Even though they don't want to miss school, they are worried it will happen again.

Gangs are a cause of gun violence in many schools, too. Fights often break out between two

Gang members listen to a former gang member, who urges them to stay away from drugs and guns.

gangs. Unfortunately, fights can quickly turn into gun battles. One boy remembers seeing guns often being waved around at his Chicago high school.

"It was over drugs, mostly," he says. "A guy would be selling in another guy's territory one day. And that's where they see each other the next day, at school. One guy makes a threat, and the other guy doesn't back down.

"It wasn't always shooting; sometimes it was just guys waving their guns around. This one guy had lots of guns in the trunk of his car. Sometimes he would open the trunk, just to scare people. He had all kinds of stuff in there—assault rifles, **sawed-off shotguns**! You'd have to be crazy to mess with that guy."[18]

Another boy agrees that gangs are armed in many schools. He was suspended several months ago for carrying a gun. He no longer brings one to school. However, he says he does not worry about rival gangs.

"I'm not scared, even though I'm not carrying [a gun]," he says. "I know I got my friends backing

Students are evacuated from a school building because of gunfire.

me up. They got guns bigger than most guys got—automatics, whatever. They're better equipped than the police."[19]

Surprise Shooters?

Gangs are not always to blame, however. Some of the most frightening examples of gun violence at school did not involve gangs. Two students in a Colorado high school murdered thirteen people. A teen shot and killed five people at his school in

A yearbook photo of one of two students who murdered thirteen people at a Colorado school.

Arkansas. A twelve-year-old killed a girl at his New Mexico middle school. The list grows longer each year.

The students responsible for these shootings were not in gangs. They were not teens who got in fights. In most cases, others were surprised to find out who was doing the shooting. One classmate of the Arkansas shooter said he didn't seem like he could do anything like that. The boy from Santee, California, seemed that way to many students, too. Said one classmate, "I can't think of why he would have done it."[20]

Were these shootings really surprising? Not to everyone, it seems. One boy told friends that he was going to kill a bunch of people. Another made up a list of people he hated, and showed it to friends. One boy even told friends about the guns he would use at school. But the friends did not tell anyone. They said they thought he was kidding. After the shooting, many of the friends felt bad that they had not told anyone.

"I should've stepped up, even if it wasn't true," says one. "That's going to be haunting me for a long time. . . . It just hurts because I could've maybe done something about it."[21]

Needing Control

But many people wonder why it happens. Teens who do not seem violent or angry suddenly make plans to kill classmates. Experts say that such

Some bullied students feel that guns give them control.

violence often starts with an unhappy person who has no control.

"No one likes to feel helpless," says one counselor. "But I see kids who feel that way all the time. They aren't noticed or respected. They may have trouble with their classes. They often have parents who have divorced, and that is very upsetting.

"Often these kids are teased, too. Maybe it's because of their size, or their weight. Maybe it's because they struggle in their classes. But they are targets for bullies. And they feel there is nothing they can do about it—no control."

The counselor continued, "but that's something a gun can do. They say, 'I'll pick up this gun. Now I've *really* got control. I can control whether someone lives or dies.' They couldn't control that they are fat or short. They couldn't control their parents' fighting. They couldn't control the bullies every day in the hallway. But at school, behind that gun, they've got that control."[22]

People know that guns don't belong in schools. But the shootings keep happening. More students are angry and have access to guns. More people are shot and killed. More lives are ruined. It's clear that for gun violence to stop, something needs to happen. But what?

Chapter Four

Looking for Answers

After a recent school shooting in a Pennsylvania town, there were some new rules. Different schools in the area wanted to make sure nothing like that happened to them. They came up with many ideas that they thought would make students and staff safer. One idea was to outlaw the backpacks many students use. Instead, students must use clear or mesh book carriers. That way, school officials could spot a student carrying a gun or a knife. Some schools have hired security police to keep watch in the halls and by the doors.

Metal Detectors

Some schools have even put in **metal detectors** by the doors. Students and others going in and out must go through the detectors. The machines are designed to beep when they sense something metal, like a gun or knife. School officials say the detectors are keeping everyone safe.

But many students don't like these changes. Some feel it's wrong for the school to outlaw their

Schools sometimes install metal detectors to detect weapons.

backpacks. They don't like metal detectors, either. They say they feel as though they are being treated like prisoners.

"We have metal detectors in my high school," says Donna. "And video cameras in the halls and out in the parking lot. It's like being in jail. Besides, they don't always work. My English teacher complains that the metal detector goes off every morning when she goes through, because of her lipstick or keys. But it didn't go off at my cousin's school when one boy brought in a gun!"[23]

Some feel that machines are not the answer. They say that children are less at risk for being shot in school than in other places they go. "Are you going to put [metal detectors] in grocery stores?" asks one woman. "Are you going to put them in every building you walk in?"[24]

Going to the Source

Instead, many people say that it's time to solve the source of gun violence. What causes the frustration and anger that leads to violence? And why are children and teens able to get their hands on guns?

Talking about making rules or limits for guns is a touchy subject. Many people feel strongly that owning a gun is their right. Others feel that guns are dangerous and should be used only by hunters, police, and soldiers. No matter what side a person believes, however, safety is very important. No one wants to see guns in the hands of children.

Some states have passed laws that require gun owners to keep guns locked up. If a teen or child uses a gun to hurt someone, the owner of the gun is responsible. He or she can be charged with the crime, since the gun was not locked away. Knowing that risk may make gun owners more careful.

In some states the law requires gun owners to lock up their guns.

Talking and listening keep parents and children connected.

Helping Troubled Kids

But guns are just part of the issue of gun violence. Anger, frustration, and fear are another part. Many experts say that adults need to take a bigger role in the lives of teens and younger children. Parents need to stay connected to their children. They need to know and care about what their children are thinking and what they are doing.

Parents need to show their children how to solve arguments, too. They can show by example how to control their temper. They can show how disagreements can be worked out peacefully. Says one parent, "Talking and listening are the key, not by yelling or slapping. And certainly not by picking up a gun and threatening someone with it."[25]

Teachers play an important role, too. "Teachers often don't know how important they are to a kid with problems," says one counselor. "Maybe the child has a troubled home life. Maybe her parents are too busy—whatever. But I know that students will often open up to a teacher about a problem before they'll talk to their own parents."[26]

One fourteen-year-old says that the adult he trusts most in the world is his English teacher. "He doesn't judge me like my parents do," he says. "And he is always telling me what a good writer I am. I let him read stuff I've written. I've never showed that stuff to anyone else. But I totally trust him. I think I could talk to him about anything."[27]

"I Felt Sick"

Some communities have started programs aimed at young people who are at risk for violence. Some of these programs show how gun violence can ruin lives. "Calling the Shots" is one that has worked in St. Paul, Minnesota.

Teens are brought to the emergency room of a hospital. The staff explains how they treat people who have been shot. But in the middle of their talk, an ambulance arrives. They see a badly injured boy

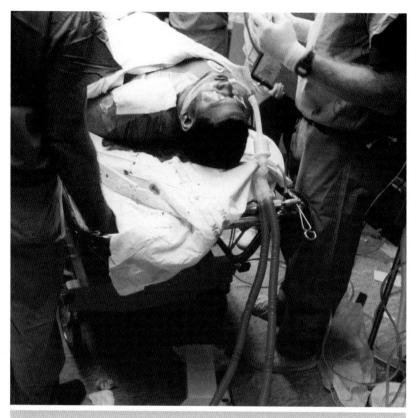

Some communities stage gunshot scenes to frighten teens at risk for violence.

arrive in an ambulance. He has been shot, and they watch doctors and nurses work on the boy. But even though they try hard to save him, he dies from his wounds. The teens then go with a doctor into the waiting room. They stand and watch while the doctor tells the parents their son is dead. And then the teens learn something else.

"We found out it was staged," says one girl. "The bloody boy, the parents, they were actors. But it was so real—I was shaking I was so afraid! Afterwards, we talked about what we felt seeing that boy. That was hard. Even the boys in our group were shaking. But the hardest part was watching the parents when they found out their son died. I felt sick, watching that. It was like, what if those were my parents?"[28]

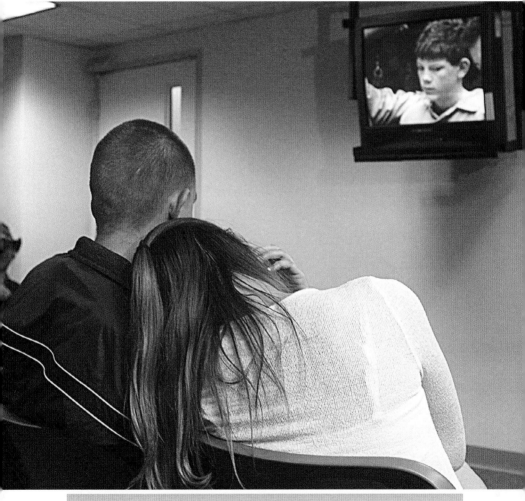

Students watch as Andy Williams appears in court.

Knowing What to Do

Many schools are helping fight gun violence, too. Police officers come to classrooms to talk about guns. They teach students what to do when a friend or classmate has a gun, or talks about shooting someone—even in a kidding way.

It is *not* smart to try to grab a gun from someone, for it might accidentally go off. The best thing to do is tell an adult quickly. It is important to understand that telling a parent or teacher about a gun is not tattling.

"We tell kids that telling about a friend who has a gun is helping, not tattling," says one police officer. "For instance, someone who decides to bring a gun to school usually tells a friend beforehand. If someone you know talks about doing that, tell an adult. Or call it in, if you want to be anonymous. Don't worry if you're not sure if they're kidding or not. It's so much better to get to the bottom of it before someone gets killed."[29]

Guns in the wrong hands are a threat to everyone. The more people learn about guns and violence, the more they can help keep schools, streets, and homes safe.

Notes

Chapter 1: "As Fast as a Bullet Can Go"

1. Personal interview, February 1999, Libby, Bloomington, MN.
2. Telephone interview, Garry, March 30, 2001.
3. Personal interview, Willie, January 1999, Minneapolis, MN.
4. Quoted in Carolyn Hoyt, "My Child Didn't Have to Die!" *McCall's*, April 1997, p. 64.
5. Telephone interview, Mike, April 11, 2001.
6. Quoted in Hoyt, "My Child Didn't Have to Die!" p. 58.

Chapter 2: The Wrong Hands

7. Personal interview, Don Jakes, April 19, 2001, Minneapolis, MN.
8. Telephone interview, Patrick, April 13, 2001.
9. Personal interview, James, March 3, 2001, St. Paul, MN.
10. Personal interview, Mary, October 1999, Minneapolis, MN.
11. Personal interview, (name withheld), April 21, 2001, (location withheld).
12. Personal interview, Xiong, November 20, 2000, Minneapolis, MN.
13. Telephone interview, Doug, April 13, 2001.

Chapter 3: Guns at School

14. Telephone interview, Kathleen, March 12, 2001.
15. Personal interview, (name withheld), November 18, 2000, (location withheld).

16. Personal interview, Dewayne, May 1998, Arden Hills, MN.

17. Personal interview, Tara, October 2000, St. Paul, MN.

18. Personal interview, (name withheld), February 1998, (location withheld).

19. Personal interview, (name withheld), February 1998, (location withheld).

20. Quoted in Ken Ellingwood and Scott Gold, "Two Killed, Thirteen Hurt in School Shooting," *Los Angeles Times*, March 5, 2001.

21. Quoted in Ellingwood and Gold, "2 Killed, 13 Hurt in School Shooting."

22. Telephone interview, Lynne, April 15, 2001.

Chapter 4: Looking for Answers

23. Personal interview, Donna, April 6, 2001, St. Paul, MN.

24. Quoted in Phuong Ly and Nahal Toosi, "Many Favor Metal Detectors," *Charlotte Observer*, August 3, 1998.

25. Lynne, April 15, 2001.

26. Lynne, April 15, 2001.

27. Personal interview, Joe, March 1998, Minneapolis, MN.

28. Personal interview, (name withheld), April 23, 2001, Brooklyn Park, MN.

29. Doug, April 15, 2001.

Glossary

auction: A source of gun-buying. Many people prefer to buy guns at auctions and gun shows, because dealers don't always follow the same rules about selling that a licensed gun dealer does.

background check: A search to see if a customer has a criminal record.

cooling-off period: The delay required in some states between applying for a gun and actually receiving it.

hit list: A list of people that a person wants to kill.

metal detector: A machine near the entrance of many schools that will alert a security guard if a gun or knife is being brought in.

sawed-off shotgun: A shotgun whose barrel has been illegally sawed off, making it easier to conceal. Sawed-off shotguns are extremely powerful weapons which are not sold by licensed gun dealers.

therapist: A trained professional who helps people deal with difficult problems in life.

For Further Exploration

Books

Jennifer Croft, *Everything You Need to Know About Guns in Your Home.* New York: Rosen, 2000. Well researched, with a good section on why people buy guns.

Gus Gedatus, *Gangs and Violence.* Mankato, MN: LifeMatters, 2000. Good section on the way gang violence affects schools.

Maryann Miller, *Working Together Against Gun Violence.* New York: Rosen, 1994. Helpful background on the legal battles about gun ownership in the United States.

Jay Schleifer, *Everything You Need to Know About Weapons in School and at Home.* New York: Rosen, 1994. Challenging reading, but very good information on positive steps children can take to create safer schools.

Websites

Handgun Control, Inc.
1225 Eye Street NW, Suite 1100
Washington, DC 20005
www.handguncontrol.org

This organization works for strict gun legislation, educating the public about the dangers of guns. They maintain a website keeping people up-to-date on laws being voted on, as well as the activities of the powerful gun lobby in Washington.

National Rifle Association (NRA)
1600 Rhode Island Avenue, NW
Washington, DC 20036
www.nra.org

Based on the idea that Americans have the right to own guns without government interference, the NRA supports responsible and effective use of guns. The organization offers the Eddie Eagle program, which teaches children safety precautions around guns.

National Safety School Center (NSSC)
4165 Thousand Oaks Blvd., Suite 290
Westlake, CA 91362
www.nssc1.org

The NSSC serves as a catalyst and advocate for the prevention of school crime and violence by providing information and resources to school principals and community police forces. The organization publishes "School Safety News Service" and also offers on-site technical help for schools experiencing problems with violence.

Youth Crime Watch
www.ycwa.org

This teen-led nonprofit organization provides information to schools and community groups on ways that teens can reduce gun violence and other crime in schools and throughout the community.

Index

About
the Author

Gail B. Stewart has written over ninety books for young people, including a series for Lucent Books called The Other America. She has written many books on historical topics such as World War I and the Warsaw ghetto.

Stewart received her undergraduate degree from Gustavus Adolphus College in St. Peter, Minnesota. She did her graduate work in English, linguistics, and curriculum study at the College of St. Thomas and the University of Minnesota. She taught English and reading for more than ten years. Stewart and her husband live in Minneapolis with their three sons.